Name

Date

IN MEMORIAM

UNABLE ARE THE LOVED TO DIE,

for love is immortality.

EMILY DICKINSON·

LIFE RECORD

Place of birth

Date of birth

Place of death

Date of death

Age

FINAL RESTING PLACE

Ceremonies by

_____

Interment in

_____

Name of cemetery

_____

Section   *Block*   *Lot*

_____

City / County / State / Province

Laid to Rest on

_____

Date

SERVICES

Officiant

Music

Bearers

Maternal

Mother

Grandmother   *Grandfather*

Great-Grandmother   *Great-Grandmother*

Great-Grandfather   *Great-Grandfather*

FAMILY TREE

Paternal

_____
Father

_____   _____
Grandmother   *Grandfather*

_____   _____
Great-Grandmother   *Great-Grandmother*

_____   _____
Great-Grandfather   *Great-Grandfather*

FAMILY RECORD

Mother

Name

Place of birth

Date of birth

Place of death

Date of death

Age

Father

Name

Place of birth

Date of birth

Place of death

Date of death

Age

FAMILY RECORD

Other Members of the Family

Siblings

Children

Grandchildren

Great-Grandchildren

DEATH IS BUT THE

next great adventure.

J.K. ROWLING

THE GRAVE ITSELF IS BUT A COVERED BRIDGE

leading from light to light,

THROUGH A BRIEF DARKNESS.

HENRY WADSWORTH LONGFELLOW

EVEN THE DARKEST NIGHT WILL END

and the sun will rise.

VICTOR HUGO

ANYTHING YOU LOSE

comes round in another form.

RUMI

LIFE IS ETERNAL;

AND LOVE IS IMMORTAL;

AND DEATH IS ONLY A HORIZON;

and a horizon is nothing
save the limit of our sight.

ROSSITER WORTHINGTON RAYMOND

WHAT IS LOVELY NEVER DIES,

BUT PASSES INTO ANOTHER LOVELINESS

star-dust or sea-foam,

flower or winged air.

THOMAS BAILEY ALDRICH

THE MOST AUTHENTIC THING ABOUT US

IS OUR CAPACITY TO CREATE, TO OVERCOME,

TO ENDURE, TO TRANSFORM, TO LOVE,

and to be greater than our suffering.

BEN OKRI

WHAT WE HAVE ONCE ENJOYED,

WE CAN NEVER LOSE.

All that we love deeply
becomes part of us.

HELEN KELLER

FOR LIFE AND DEATH ARE ONE,

*even as the river and
the sea are one.*

KAHLIL GIBRAN

WHEN ONE MAN DIES,
ONE CHAPTER IS NOT TORN
OUT OF THE BOOK,
*but translated into a
better language.*

JOHN DONNE

All rights reserved.
Published in the United States by Clarkson Potter/Publishers,
an imprint of the Crown Publishing Group, a division of
Penguin Random House LLC, New York.
crownpublishing.com
clarksonpotter.com

CLARKSON POTTER is a trademark and POTTER with
colophon is a registered trademark of Penguin Random House LLC.

978-1-9848-2266-6

Printed in China

Book design by Nicole Block and Danielle Deschenes
Patterns by Shutterstock © Curly Pat; Rodina Olena (first
appearance on page 18)

10 9 8 7 6 5 4 3 2 1

First Edition